Into My Life

Into My Life

Dr. Alaa Zidan

PARTRIDGE

To order additional copies of this book, contact
Toll Free 800 101 2657 (Singapore)
Toll Free 1 800 81 7340 (Malaysia)
orders.singapore@partridgepublishing.com

www.partridgepublishing.com/singapore

Contents

"Into my life represents my own views and opinions without any bias or fulfilling certain agenda, this is just my own reflections and part of my ongoing story and journey I hope you like it."

Dr. Alaa Zidan

Mission Statement

Whenever I associate with anyone, may I think myself the lowest among all and hold the other supreme in depth of my heart.

When I see beings of wicked nature, pressed by violent sins and affiliations, may I hold these rare ones dear as if I had a precious treasure.

When others out of envy, treat me badly with abuse, slander and dislike, may I suffer the defeat and offer the victory to others.

When the one whom I benefited with great hope and love, hurts me badly, may I behold him as my Inspiration and supreme Guru.

In nutshell may I directly and indirectly offer benefit, happiness, and Love to all beings, may I secretly take upon myself the harm and suffering of all beings.

Bless me God with the Energy to serve and send all beings unconditional Love."

Alaa Zidan

Acknowledgment

I would like to convey my deepest gratitude's to everyone who helped to bring this work to light, especially my soul mate, partner, sweet heart and my love **Hala Charfuddine**, she was extremely patient with me and encouraged me round the clock to write this book

I have a lot of other people who inspired me and stimulated me to carry on with my work, the marvelous group of NGN International, Bahrain, they were so supportive to me all the time.

A special tribute and thanks to my late great mother and my two brilliant sisters **SaFaa** and **Naglaa,** and The Charafuddines, Mainly Basem, Noor.., Ghaleb, Saed Amal and Lyala my beautiful mother in law who is a true mother to me

I couldn't be what I am without the help of my mentors, Mona and Namir George**,** and my friend Hisham Toson, Hanan Janahi and Islam Kamal

so thank you from the bottom of my heart, may I wish to all who helped, inspired, encouraged and hurt me all the best and a joyful blissful life.

Dr. Alaa Zidan
20/2/2016

A tribute to my Lovely Sister Safaa

My heart is aching with the death of my sister Safaa, is it loss, sadness, grief, darkness,

I really don't know, all what I feel is my heart has been ripped off my chest through a crushed wound that has no surgical principles to treat or save lives in fact it is a wound that meant to kill and it did, when I will survive that I have no clue, but I truly believe that I haven't felt such a grief in my life with such a profound intensity except for the loss of my mother, a web of darkness is entangling and haunting me every moment every breath I take is heavy, my eyes are dry as there are no tears left to shed.

I learned from this terrible experience that everything is done for a good reason the supreme consciousness, the source, the creator the supreme intelligence has its own ways that we might not comprehend nor appreciate except when we look closer to the universe around us, I can understand the magnitude and the intensity of my grief due to the love that I feel for my sister, but if I remained like this paralyzed within the web of darkness then this means that all what I feel for my sister is just a sense of possession that brings joy to my life but this cannot be love, again this defeats what I truly feel for my sister which is unconditional love.

She was a very influential figure in my life, a source of kindness and compassion and she was a mother to me, she stands very firm for what she believes with no hesitation or doubt.

Safaa had a very profound statement when she praised my performance while treating the injured during the events that took place in Bahrain some 5 years ago when she kept saying to her two lovely kids that your uncle is a true hero and I am honored to be his sister.

She never spared any effort in supporting me unconditionally with her pleasant clear personality, caring attitude and compassionate empathetic approach in her life.

For the past four years I was and remained close to her, by sparing no effort in visiting and staying with her beautiful family in Orlando, she cooked and shopped for me with exquisite style, novelty and Joy.

She was a ball of light, she loved me and I loved her may god bless and rest her soul.

My Dear Safaa you haven't left us in fact your body is absent but your soul is always with us I do see you winking and smiling to me indicating how pleased and comfortable you are, Love You…

Alaa Zidan
12/12/2013

A Tribute to Safaa from my sister Naglaa

Me and Safaa grow up in a tiny apartment our room was very very tiny you could hardly walk in it consist of a bed a couch a desk a closet the couch was full of books I never was able to sleep on it Safaa studied on the desk me in the couch we shared the same cloth the same bed the closet my mother trailer all our cloth we had amazing food clean house we never had money for a taxi so me a Safaa enjoyed the 35 minute walk every morning to medical school how much I miss it all laughs and stories we shared we excelled academically surprised every one and we passed the American Medical License Exam with high grades how much I miss my sister.

Naglaa Zidan
18/3/2016

Introduction

IN TO MY LIFE

We should rejoice for any problems that face us, we are blessed with an open menu unlimited and unconditioned from the source this menu keeps us focusing on the solutions, examining our options and adjusting our life to accommodate harmony and balance.

For those who don't know me, let me introduce myself, I am a human obsessed with spreading the only message that truly counts which is love and dedicating my life for this very reason, for me love is the given gift to all humans who keeps us surviving, living and enjoying, it is the true solution to most if not all your adversities, I might sound naïve or out of touch or a lunatic and believe me, when I learned that love is all what you have got, then I might as well love, love and love from my heart, people would think that you are a kind of an alien who is not realistic or that I might be under the influence of drugs, but this is the reality we are creatures gifted with love, so why should we waste such an unlimited, unconditioned, abundant energy, we are meant to love and be loved, we should begin by loving ourselves, by enjoying the fact that every moment pass by is a gift, a victory and a bless.

I never held any grudge, nor hatred probably once in a blue Moon, I might be angry after all, I am human but I never get myself entangled in a web of hatred and vengeance, I learned my lesson and I knew that I can waste my life if I surrendered to the web of hatred and vengeance.

The starting point is to love yourself, enjoy life even dance, smile, one of my daily rituals is that I love always to greet strangers and I always do that for 5 persons whether they are men, women or kids, such an amazing feeling when you greet strangers and they respond back, I hardly experienced anyone who didn't greet me in return, a simple smile breaks the ice, unleashes your waves of light and spreads love, it should be done spontaneously, unplugged and from your heart.

For those who think that this can only be applied in fiction and movies, I prove them that they are cocooned in a shell of fear, why don't you try, that believe me it can change your life, when you travel to a place where people don't speak your language and you cant speak theirs, you smile and they smile back, smile is the most impressive, positive and brilliant method of communication, and by the way smile boosts your positive energy and makes it contagious among others who are haunted in being formal as an image of seriousness and Authority.

Being grumpy, angry and sarcastic doesn't stain or label you as a tough leader or a serious manager.

Being angry doesn't turn you in a competent person, or a successful leader or a powerful president, in fact it turns you in to someone who never appreciate the gifts that he owns and missing the true life.

What I mean by true life is a life with purpose that makes you move and trembles with joy and bliss., A purpose which is compelling represents who you are and what you want.

Having the courage to declare and believe in what you are is the essence of a purposeful life a life that has a vision, mission and passion coupled with volition.

This book is not a sequel of my first one which is my own reflections, it is my own life that shows what happened to me from 2011 till the present, exploring several events that took place, and changed my life.

bragging about the past, conditions that made you not what you truly want is mere failure that provides a suitable recipe for escaping from reality, we create our own reality, if you think negative you will end negative attracting negative energy result in negative impacts, being sad feeling sorry for yourself, judging people, comparing yourself with others, envying other people successes, and proclaiming that you are hurt with other people acts all of these are just excuses created by your mind, to play trick on you and showing that you are right in doing that, but that is all a false and unnatural,

Dr. Alaa Zidan

we have to embrace life with its ups and downs, that is the challenge that creates and generates opportunities.

We are surrounded with a lot of blesses and gifts provided to us ready made, we need to use it to the maximum, it is like driving a beautiful car but not exploring all its options and ignoring its potentials.

We should never think low of ourselves, when we do that I call it the brink of darkness, as we are ignoring what have been provided by the divine supreme source and that is why we cant perceive the beauty around us all the time, as if we deny the existence of the source, the divine, the creator.

Chapter 1

Arab spring and Egypt

The young generation in Egypt, impressed me for several reasons, they made the impossible possible, they became the voice of the voiceless with courage, perseverance, love, determination and over and above they defended the basic human rights which is, freedom and social justice.

Thank you young Egyptians who were able to unite whole Egypt under a compelling cause and a sacred message which is freedom from Tyranny.

The young Egyptians revived my sole and created a meaning for life, I salute them and bow to their courage and I am truly grateful to all who shared in January 25 Revolution and June 30 as well, the only Country that started 2 revolutions for the sake of Egypt, this Revolution is a master piece that is taught in the most prestigious political institutes all around the world and the message is no one no matter who he is can challenge the masses.

Now at the present moment I am re-exploring what this revolution brought to us and I am not pessimistic nor skeptical in addressing such an outstanding event that changed the face of Egypt and history.

Are we better than before January 25? For the time being in the start of 2016 the answer to my question is definitely No, the people mindset has changed to be free but the state itself is corrupt and it never changed the state institutes in Egypt needs complete revamping to be injected with the vision of young generation, more imagination, clear vision, dedication and commitment.

We can not accept the same technocrats who were in the Era of the previous presidents to run the country with their old, wrinkled mindset and their stagnate system, if you look closely to the problems facing Egypt the solutions remain the same as before nothing has changed, corruption nests in every corner in the state and governmental institutes, in fact security is extremely brutal with frequent human right abuses, level of illiteracy is sky rocketing, health care is a disaster, and education is far inferior to our expectations,

The first elected president was a failure and the current president is on the verge of being a prophet or a pharaoh and that is our main problem is that we address the president as being someone superior, a god who is beyond criticism and above all the same old story the current president after nearly 20 months while he is in power he did some ambitious projects such as the new Suez Canal which will have a long term benefit yet such ambitious projects the benefits are not felt by the people because it take time

Our President need to know very well and I never doubted your intelligence nor your love to Egypt and your patriotism and I have the reason to believe that our freedom evolves from raising our opinion and expressing our difference even to the president because no one above constructive criticism.

The presidency is the top post in serving people a servant of Egyptians with a four-year contract, and it is rational when we are aware that if the president prove Success and implemented a clear strategy to establish a modern civil democratic country then he might be reelected, but if not then there is no reason to continue.

We need Deeds not sweet words and, declaring promises that you never kept

To be a civil modern country, The president need to cartel the religion clergy who generates fundamentalism and terrorism, instead of talking and talking about renewing the religion preaching, those religion clergy are the source of terrorism, you need to totally change the Religion syllabus in schools and faculties, we need to encourage the ability to think, debate and discuss our religion and explain and elaborate and stress on the true message of Islam which is Peace, Islam has nothing to do with blood shed and violence, but the clergy who are incompetent, bribed by their Wahhabi masters are the head of the viper. And that will be the road of enlightenment

So when you Deal with Terrorism our President is only combating terrorist but not the terrorism as a phenomena and concept you have to start to deal with the concepts and ideas that generate Terrorism.

When it comes to Health care and Education Egypt under you became top of the list of failures in Education and health care.

How can you claim that you are setting the foundation of a civil modern democratic country and people are locked in prisons for thinking or debating their uncertainty about the poisons injected by religion clergy and expressing their views?

How can you be civil country and you are a top listed country in breaching the very basics of human rights

How can you claim democracy while the young generation who ignited the Revolution are locked in prisons and tortured, shame on every Egyptian who accept those grave acts, you are The Egyptian president loved by all but you turned into a sweet talker who is confused and preoccupied in changing his face instead of his country, I believe that you are the luckiest guy to run Egypt, I cant remember any president before you who had such an overwhelming popularity with the exception of Nasser, but unfortunately you are on the wrong path and it is never to late to correct, and review your decisions and acts.

What is needed to be done? We need imagination, clear visions and intelligence to restore Egypt to its deserved position as A Beacon of enlightenment and the source of culture and modernization.

We need young and new blood with their unbeatable passion and stamina to be in charge, to have their chance in initiating creativity and innovation, we need to dismantle the technocrat system that propagates corruption and promote disruption

We need to revamp the education and Health care to meet people expectations.

We need to be independent from any control not slaves to any country

We need to combat Radicalism, fundamentalism and Wahhabism as a concept and that is the core to eliminate terrorism

I am expressing my views and I am never inclined to attack anyone on the contrary, I am worried about my country and I am setting an example of a simple Egyptian Doctor who spare no effort, fear no one in declaring my thoughts, expressing my concepts maybe one day such thoughts can be translated into actions for my beloved EGYPT.

Imprisoning scholars, thinkers, writes and creative philosophers is against the essence of establishing a democratic civil state, I find it extremely uncivilized act to imprison a person who focus on using the mind in understanding the depth of our great religion Islam, someone who is trying to reach the core of Islam, not through the rigid conservative closed minded explanation of the clergy to the narratives and old explanations that rhetoric are using since several hundred years, our enlightened scholars are honored with the true Islam that is established on a strong foundation of peace, compassion and love, our Islam that honors human The Brilliant Islam which is build on the fact that we are all one, Our enlightened scholars are accused by defaming religion and based on a 1 defaming religion legislation they are imprisoned, the irony is that this legislation is unconstitutional.

There is such a deep gap and emerging contradiction between what our president claims or hopes and what is going on in reality this gap is increasing and that creates contradictions and lack of trust.

The Security in Egypt is using Iron Fist, on daily basis we see torturing, abusing people by the security, if we read the history properly and learn from our mistakes we can see over the past centuries that states and countries has fallen down due to Tyranny and the control of security over all aspects of life.

The core reasons of all revolutions through the whole history stems from the control of security, Egyptians started two revolutions not for economic reasons but for freedom, and dignity

Complaining about a problem without posing a solution is whining and I have no intention to whine what so ever but I introduced my own reflections and suggested solutions to be shared, discussed for the sake of my Beloved EGYPT.

I might sound a bite Harsh on our President, knowing that he is in charge of country overwhelmed with deep seated problems since 60 years, but I never been Rude at all because

Rudeness is the weak person imitation of strength, and I never been weak in my life.

we should be honest in voicing our opinions in this new Era and we shouldn't be slaves to anyone who imprison my thoughts, drown my creativity and kill my ambition.

We cannot become what we want by remaining what we are, we should change and embrace change by all means, at the beginning change is extremely difficult and it becomes more and more difficult, at the end it is brilliant, and that is life, life is never about being risk free or secure because that is against our very basic nature

I believe to start solving our problems we should and must embrace change., eventually all will fall into place till then, laugh, and dance at the confusion, live for the present moment and be aware that everything happens for a good reason.

I believe that our core problems arise from being overwhelmed and busy to make a living and forgetting to make a true life.

Being strong is to love, and radiate happiness when we are unhappy, to forgive, to be calm and silent in moments of despair, to generate joy when we can't smile, to make someone happy when you have a broken heart and to have faith when you no longer believe.

The moment you start loving yourself you will stop hurting others, the universe is in you, look inside your true self and everything you want, you already are.

One of the hardest lessons in life is to let go anger, vengeance, loss and change as we know is never easy, we really fight to hang on and also we fight to let go. as the secret of happiness is accepting who and where you are and making the best of every given moment.

Life is not about finding your true self it is about creating yourself.

And don't let someone dim your radiant light and glow because it is shinning in the eyes of others. You may not be able to control all the events around you but remember that you should never be reduced by these events mainly by visualizing yourself as a floating ball in the sea, it reflects harmony and balance, when the sea is smooth with no waves, and even in adverse conditions with high waves the ball sinks momentarily but again it resurface back.

Never explain yourself to any one, you don't need anyone's s blessing nor approvals as it is not important what people think of you what really counts is what you think of yourself. Always be your self express yourself have faith in yourself that is your victory.

If you speak badly about yourself, by being harsh as this will undermine the warrior within you, because we are warriors of light,

A warrior of light serves, speaks from his heart, stands for what he believes, never badmouth any one, serves and love unconditionally.

A warrior of light crosses hurdles, embrace fear, hugs risks and radiate light that sets a roadmap for what he truly wants. Creating the life that feels good in the inside not that looks nice from outside.

Chapter 2

Warrior of light

A warrior of light is someone who don't have to hate, simply because he is busy loving people,

A warrior of light inspire, leads without a title, fearless and he never quit.

A warrior of light is success seeker, not a failure avoider

A warrior of light never stops doing his best because no one is giving the credit.

A warrior of light Embraces change, touch people hearts by showing them how amazing they are.

A warrior of light defends but not offend, practice what he preaches

A warrior of light unite but not divide,

A warrior of light has the guts to do what is needed not what is convenient, makes progress rather than finding excuses.

A warrior of light is compassionate, grateful and makes a difference in people life.

A warrior of light is encircled with strings of intelligence, creativity and imagination

A warrior of light, enjoys life, bashes fear, dances and live like a child.

A warrior of light never allow fear to stop him from growing.

A warrior of light evolves and progress.

A warrior of light never gets old because he learns every day, once he is learning he is always young and vibrant

A warrior of light is never too old to set another goals and dreams another new dream.

A warrior of light never gives up he can do anything but never everything.

A warrior of light follows his heart and he is aware about the worse battle between what he knows and what he feels.

A warrior of light knows that gratitude creates joy.

A warrior of light speaks honestly, thinks sincerely, and acts with integrity

A warrior of light knows that his happiest moments when he loses himself in serving others.

A warrior of light works hard in silence, letting his success makes the noise

A warrior of light expects nothing, and appreciate everything, he knows that expectations hurt.

A warrior of light doesn't expect anything in exchange of the love that he gives.

A warrior of light focus on the good.

A warrior of light knows very well that gratitude is like a muscle the more you practice it the more you grow.

A warrior of light is the king of comebacks. And he converts his setbacks into opportunities.

A warrior of light meets real tragedy in life by using the challenge to find his inner strength.

A warrior of light Makes sure that his behavior and Actions reflects what he truly believes

A warrior of light is fully restored to the blessed moment of serenity

A warrior of light is fully focused on the present moment

A warrior of light is open and receptive to abundance and prosperity.

A Warrior of light is proud of his setbacks enjoys being himself because he knows that no one can be better than himself except himself

A warrior of light is full of love, enjoys life, Adores & inspire people

A warrior of light never gives up he loves his scares coz it reminds him how courageous he is.

Warrior of light knows that before being Muslim Egyptian & doctor he knows that he should be Human
Warrior of light love forgive and enjoy he never judge nor compare

A warrior of light has no grudge against those who hurt him he loves them coz they unleashed his excellence

Chapter 3

Doubts in Frankfurt

I had a moving conversation with the love of my life My wife Hala in Frankfurt Airport on our way to Orlando before few month, and I was telling her I don't know why this time I feel that I always truly love Bahrain from my Heart but does Bahrain love me ? the minute I posed this question I started a gush of ideas and reflections and my mind played me for few minutes and this was one of the rare moments that my mind kept playing with me, tricking me and injecting extremely dark and negative thoughts deceiving and even controlling me, actually when I am talking about Mind, I mean the thoughts that keep barging in the mind.

I was so emotional, sensitive, and tears kept pouring from my eyes

Why I am thinking in this negative way, it never happened to me since, I have been trained as a competent spiritual and energy healer, but I am a human and things happen but it was a turning point in my life why?

I knew that life is and will be always a mixtures of good and bad moments, I have to accept that, but the main reason that

I felt for a flicker of moment that I am not loved by Bahrain was due to cumulative effects of a strand of incidents that took place in my life.

I am a proud Egyptian and always will be, but I wanted to be a holder of a Bahraini passport which will be a great honor to me, I do definitely deserve such an honor for serving Bahrain for over 20 years of my life, My wife is Bahraini and I am not, that creates a sense of separation in my feeling why is that, but taking it from the positive aspect, I belong to a family that I call the league of nations, My wife is Bahraini and originally Lebanese, I am Egyptian and I might be an American my sister is American, and my kids are Canadians, such a mix of nationalities reflects only one true fact from the very beginning of mankind which is that we are all one, and we are all strings in this beautiful universal fabric.

If I hold a Bahraini passport does this means that Bahrain loves me officially I would say YES, but spiritually and morally the issue has more profound depth, its about feelings, sensations and emotions and once uncertainty and doubts haunts me that was a serious issue and with the Support and love of people surrounding me I conquered this negative feeling that was in me for few minutes.

Mindfulness, meditation and focusing on the present moment was my unique personal recipe to erase such a feeling that never recurred.

We should never compare nor judge others, I am not a judge nor a god, I have no right to judge others, I have no right to feel sorry for myself.

I am blessed with the most beautiful lady in my eyes the love of my life, my guarding angel, my savior and ultimate supporter so I rejoice such a bless and a gift.

Every thing happens for a good reason,

Forgive me my Bahrain for doubting your love to me, I am truly sorry for that it was just a feeling that kept haunting me for few moments.

Forgive me Bahrain for forgetting how you made me to I became what I am

Forgive me Bahrain for letting uncertainty cloud my thoughts and crumble my positivity

Forgive me Bahrain for not doing my best in very few occasions that I even can not recall.

Forgive Bahrain that I forgot that you made me a HERO

Forgive me Bahrain that I Forgot that you turned me in a popular figure

Forgive me Bahrain that I forgot that you were the reason of my boom as a Doctor, healer, teacher and a motivator

I am proud and honored that I represented my Bahrain in plenty of international conferences which turned me in one of the well known motivating speakers, forgive me Bahrain for forgetting that.

Forgive me Bahrain because I forgot that I was blessed and provided with the woman that bared me happiness and an adorable family in Bahrain and she is a Bahraini born in Bahrain.

My love to Bahrain will remain ever and forever unconditional and with no shred of a doubt, and when my time comes I would be honored to be buried in My Bahrain and in Sitra Island as I worked in this Area for around five years where I was truly loved by people there.

So please My Bahrain when my time comes burry me in your arms, embrace me and remember me as one of your dearest sons.

Chapter 4

My Passion

All my life, I have been searching, reflecting and questioning my true passion, what is the real true thing that Awa me an and keep my heart pumping and overwhelms me with the feeling of freedom and joy. And I found what sets me free.

Serving people, through motivating, healing and teaching, when I teach I truly enjoy it it flows spontaneously from my heart and the best performance comes from the heart, no matter who and what I teach, I motivate my candidates, students and I heal them through encouragement and motivation, I don't only teach the material, I talk about my experience in life, my stories.

storytelling is considered to be one of the most inspirational and compelling methods of successful communication.

Teaching helps me to be connected to my candidates, engaging them, and enhancing open discussions beyond the academic content of any course that I teach, their feedback about my teaching is always beyond my own expectations and that what truly drives me to improve and excel in my teaching techniques

I have the reason to believe that teaching healed me before I healed others, helped me before I help others and served me in aligning my potentials and setting my style to serve and teach my students, so in nutshell Teaching changed my life from different prospective and changed me to be more innovative, creative and Imaginative.

Teaching enhanced my intelligence through knowing that intelligence is not about knowledge only but it is mainly about imagination.

During my darkest moments, I always find teaching is an outlet that vents my emotions, feeling unleash my energy and enhance and boost my mood it is my ultimate therapy that treats me from being trapped in the web of darkness and negativity, it is the light that show me the path of my life, it is the guide that enlightens me, Teaching is always been and will remain my therapy to remedy me from the pathology of the mind.

Chapter 5

A Recipe of Compassion

We all enter into the realm of friendship with the intention of enjoying ourselves and one another in a partnership and yet, when misunderstandings arise and we aren't feeling connected with our partner, our default mode is usually to lash out at them or to shut down and go inside. The key to overcoming this and to prevent sabotaging our relationships is emotional intelligence—and a fundamental component of emotional intelligence is *compassion*.

compassion is a feeling of deep Empathy for another who is stricken by misfortune, accompanied by a strong desire to alleviate the suffering. Without being attached to the outcome

To be compassionate in our relationship means that we are able to recognize when our partner or spouse is suffering in some way and to be loving and kind to them as they move through their process. This kind of support can be provided in a number of ways.

Let's consider basic human needs, as taught by psychologist Abraham Maslow. All of our behaviors are driven by our needs, and our needs are derived from our emotional states. After our needs of food and shelter have been met, each of us have very important basic needs—four of which are the need for attention, affection, appreciation, and acceptance. The ways in which we seek these things is dependent upon our level of emotional intelligence, our beliefs, and our core values. Following are some examples of how you can bring awareness to these areas and begin to practice being more compassionate in your relationship.

Attention

We all need attention—to feel seen, heard, and recognized. We need to know that we matter and that we are a part of a greater collective. Think about the ways in which you need and seek attention each day, and consider how you might provide this need for attention for your partner.

Listen with Intention

One way to be attentive toward your partner is to minimize distractions so that you can be completely present with them. Turn toward them and listen with the intention of really hearing what they are saying. Try listening with your heart rather than your mind when your partner is expressing themselves. Let them finish sharing their thoughts and feelings before interjecting your opinion or your solution, or going back to whatever you were working on. Often times, people just need to be paid attention to and feel heard.

Affection

Everyone needs some level of affection, including those who aren't necessarily the touchy-feely types. Affection comes in many forms, including a sincere smile, a kind gesture, a gentle touch on the arm, giving hugs, or making love. You can also be affectionate in your speech by using soft tones, encouraging words, and compliments.

Be Kind with Your Speech

Sometimes it's not *what* we say but, rather, *how* we say things. Take a moment to really consider what your partner is going through and speak to them with loving kindness. Consider a time when you were going through something similar and see how you might support your partner in a way that would have felt good for you in your own time of need.

If what they are experiencing is affecting you in a negative way, you may want to contemplate what you're feeling inclined to say to them before doing so. Run your communication through these questions in your mind prior to verbalizing it: Is it true? Is it necessary? Is it kind? Do I want to be right or do I want to have peace?

Appreciation

Every one has an innate need to feel valued and appreciated, especially by those we love. Find ways to show your appreciation for your partner by acknowledging their actions and being thoughtful about ordinary matters. Try to put yourself in your partner's shoes and imagine what their reality is like to help you better understand where they are at. Emotionally intelligent couples are intimately familiar with each other's world and they take the time to bask in their appreciation for one another. Consider the qualities and characteristics of your partner that you genuinely appreciate and share these things with them frequently.

Nurture Your Friendship and Your Relationship

Successful relationships all have a solid friendship at their core, which points to the individuals having a mutual respect for and an enjoyment of each other's company as a foundational component. They don't just get along, there is a fondness and an admiration for one another and they also support each other's hopes and aspirations. It's also highly productive to spend time having conversations about shared meaningful experiences on a regular basis.

Acceptance

As individuals, we all share an imperative need to feel accepted by our partners and in our daily lives. It's easy to accept those aspects of ourselves and others that are beautiful, inspiring, happy, and successful. Where the real challenge lies is accepting ourselves and others' not-so-desirable qualities.

Create a Safe Space for Your Partner to Be Themselves

Creating a safe environment for your partner to be vulnerable and share themselves fully. Let them know how much you care for them and that you have no judgment toward anything they may be thinking or feeling, and that they are perfect just as they are. None of us are exempt from embodying behaviors, qualities, or characteristics that are less than desirable.

Whenever you are feeling charged up about someone else's behavior, ask yourself: *Where have I demonstrated this type of behavior in my own life?* It won't take much digging to find where we all have the capacity to exercise poor judgment and to make mistakes. The gift in recognizing this is that we are able to glean the lesson or wisdom from those qualities and use them in positive ways. By recognizing that we all share in this experience at some point or another, it helps us soften into supporting another when they are in a place of suffering or need. Tell your partner all the ways in which you appreciate and accept them for who and what they are—exactly as they are.

Sometimes it's difficult to remain in a compassionate place with our partners. It requires a level of awareness and emotional intelligence that, at times, can seem far-reaching. You will always have some complaints about your partner and vice versa. Catching yourself before you go to a place of criticism or defensiveness and pausing for a moment can be just the thing you need to redirect your focus toward compassion for your partner. Bring yourself back to all the positive things about your relationship and wait until you're both in a good space before discussing challenges. From this space, you can work together to set course corrections and design conscious and loving recovery strategies.

Chapter 6

Wisdom

Wisdom is build through a gradual and slow fashion, it reminds me when you see a drop of water keeps trickling on a hard steel till it goes into metal failure and breaks, the drops of water trickling are a mixture of love, gratitude, and compassion that builds up wisdom and obviously the steel is our heart, my point is such a buildup of wisdom comes from not only practice, but from deliberate practice that leads to mastery and that is why it takes hard work and time to build up your wisdom and it is never been a thankless task, it is a task that is worth doing and practicing it on daily basis.

I believe that calling myself a healer is over rated, because We all have the potentials and means to heal ourselves from within all what I do is to enable people to discover their gold mine and gifts and endless menu of brilliant tools to heal themselves.

I always pay my tribute and utmost respects for all who helped and taught me the art of healing or enabling people to heal themselves and who tops my list is **My Wife Hala**

This is the lady that bared me happiness, joy and bliss, with her love and compassion she empowered, supported and believed in me, a true Ball of light an intense energy of giving and serving.

A warrior of light that stands for what she believes, inspires me with her witty character, she is my savior, and my life spiritual consultant, Hala s mission in life is to serve all, she never judges, nor compare.

She is the love of my life

my close friend Mona a princess who learned the secrete and won her battle against multiple sclerosis, she always told me that Alaa you are a master in the Art of helping and serving people and causes, keep up the good work, she always claims that she learned from me more than I learned from her and that what I call wisdom.

Mona crushed all the hurdles and adversities in her life, no matter how many problems she faces, she always impresses me with her light,

Thank you Mona for believing in me, thank you Mona for all the moments that you spend to coach and mentor me, I am thankful, and grateful for all the wisdom that you provided.

Then comes Namir My best friend a brilliant teacher in the Domain of Health and safety

Such an admirable person, a pure heart like a child and a walking Wikipedia in knowledge the beauty about Namir is that he never ever hesitates in serving and dispersing his knowledge round the clock to everyone, such a rare caliber in these days, with his sweet personality and compassionate heart I would say I am blessed with his inspirational friendship.

Chapter 7

Rebel

I love being a rebel, because a Rebel speaks his heart

A rebel is spontaneous

A rebel never controls or like to be controlled

A rebel is free, freedom is his temple

A rebel is fearless

A rebel never rules or be ruled

A rebel Embrace change and adores risk because he is aware that a risky life is a riskless life.

A rebel enjoys serving, and he never bother with titles

A rebel enjoys life, dance, rejoice and lives the present moment

A rebel never ages because he learns round the clock, the moment he starts learning he is always young.

A rebel never gives up.

A rebel is patient, determined and enthusiastic.

A rebel never gossips, nor back stab because he is above all that

A rebel never wastes his time.

A rebel respects, understands and accept others

A rebel loves his enemies, because they ignite his believes and passion

A rebel has a vision, mission and a statement of intent

Let me share with you my own statement of intent that I always declare to my students

"We are the people who serve, train and develop you to become a team player in the community We are the training servants that enable you to unleash your creativity and innovation we are your eyes and ears that see and listen to your problems.

We are your tools who enable you to focus, and love what you do and do what you love We are born to serve you because we envision you as a success seeker not a failure avoider

We are your pillars instruments and means to generate compassion, gratitude and love

We are your path on being a future influencer and a true leader"

Behind me is infinite power, before me is endless possibility and around me is boundless opportunity.

Challenges are what make life interesting. Overcoming them is what makes life meaningful.

Chapter 8

Collection of my beautiful tweets

Freedom is a choice

Freedom is change.

Freedom is life. Life is meaningless without freedom

Freedom is the nucleus of love cell,

Freedom is the energy that generates light and joy

Freedom is the source and the center of existence

Freedom is love and compassion

Freedom is courage

Freedom is standing for what you believe

Freedom is about unlocking the chains of mediocrity, dogmatism and fixed belief systems

Freedom is about gratitude

Freedom is the eraser of concept of eliminating other cultures and religions

Freedom is about rejoicing and respecting other cultures and religions

No one can deprive my freedom unless I give him the consent

Freedom is the essence and fragrance of life

Chapter 9

Relinquishments

Relinquish the need to control

Relinquish the need to live for others expectations

Relinquish your fixed, stoned and limited beliefs systems

Relinquish feeling sorry for yourself

Relinquish bragging and complaining

Relinquish your attachments

Relinquish your clutter

Relinquish your past

Relinquish your excuses

Relinquish fear

Relinquish Anger

Relinquish Judgment

Relinquish the resistance to change

Relinquish blaming others

Relinquish defeating yourself

Relinquish titles and labels

Relinquish being harsh on yourself

Relinquish putting people down, your strength lies in lifting people up.

Relinquish being an intellect, by exercising your intelligence and imagination

Relinquish violence and embrace peace

Relinquish envy and hatred and empower yourself by forgiveness

Relinquish overthinking as you can create a problem that doesn't exist from the start

Relinquish your ego by doing exactly what you fear.

Relinquish being average and always be the best version of yourself.

Relinquish complexity and seek simplicity.

Relinquish being conceited and seek humbleness

Relinquish bad words and make sure to taste your words before spitting them out

Relinquish living in the comfort zone and know that the false safety and the seduction of the comfort zone is more devastating than leading a risky life and the dangers of the unknown

Relinquish being a follower of the crowd and raise your standards

Relinquish being an average and always be a first a class

Relinquish being busy and focus on productivity

Relinquish mediocrity and focus on mastery

Relinquish Delusions and focus on execution

Relinquish energy vampires and embrace discipline and protect your energy

Relinquish energy of lack and open yourself to abundance and prosperity

Relinquish complacency and invest in educating yourself.

Relinquish those who doubt your greatness

Relinquish being a failure avoider and be a success magnate

Relinquish sadness and celebrate your greatness

Your past Never defines your future because we create our own reality

Chapter 10

Religion

Religion is one of the most sensitive issues and topics that I will address and again, I repeat that what I am writing reflects my own personal views without attacking any concepts, ideas or persons.

I am born free and freedom is my choice, and I am entitled to voice my opinion,

I believe that Religion is something that ought to be properly understood, perceived and addressed, it is something impressive to believe in God, or Allah or, the divine whatever you love to call, the universe has been created by a supreme force, by the divine intelligence, by the source the creator and I am addressing this religion issue.

Because there is unnecessary pointless attack against religion by the militant atheists claiming that the main source of regression, lack of prosperity, deprivation, blood shed and rains of violence all around the world is religion,

I believe that the Religion clergy are the one responsible, coupled with the ignorance of the people who are thriving to be followers of the crowds, also there are a lot of other cumulative factors to blame but not religion,

the religion clergy explores and explains within their intellectual limits the content and the texts without in-depth explanation of the symbolic meaning and the real context turning there way of thinking into a nasty control system that paved the way to institutionalize religion by creating figures, churches and mosques to be the only vessel of true religion from their perspective erasing our ability to discuss, debate, understand and question their explanation and eroding our capability of enlightenment and thus a control system created added to the fixed beliefs since childhood our minds became imprisoned by prison wardens and those are the priests, the sheiks, Mullahs and pops, they want to dismantle our ability to reflect and question, they want to erase our courage to doubt and think, I believe the more the doors of enlightenment are opened the more we will be religious, but I can not be a follower to radicalism that concepts that is based on eliminating other ways of thinking and reflecting, creating a culture of blame hatred enhancing violence, separation and discrimination because the main drive is the Bedouin, Deseret, emotionless, hard and eliminative culture., Wahhabism is a fascist movement because it eliminates other religions and judge people faith from an extremely superficial dimension that depends on the image of a Muslim from outside, if he is growing a beard with a just above the ankle dress, then you are a true Muslim and you keep twisting the world into struggle which is Jihad and explain it to take the form of blood shed, violence and killing those who are not Muslims,

I believe that would be the core of Religion fascism and that Wahhabi Salafist Dark approach is the inspiration of Terrorism, all what ISIS do from mass killing non Muslims, beheading and burning non Muslims and raping non Muslim women, enslaving and selling them is mentioned in the books of Wahhabism and that is the main production source and pipeline of terrorist, through the mind control of young ignorant people who can easily manipulated by creating the concept of being a martyr in the Name of Allah for the sake of heaven and beautiful angels.

If you look around you and you closely examine the centers of disputes, conflicts and war, you will find that the Arab region is the front runner, because Arab countries didn't perceive till this very moment, is that sectorial conflicts are the core of such wars that almost regressed this region 100 years in the Dark ages, because that reflects that we Arabs lack the sense of belonging, we never read, and we are probably a minority among Arabs are elite and educated but by no means they cane initiate progress in their communities because they are intellect and they never used their intelligence, they lack the vision and imagination.

These elite in our Arab world couldn't feel the pulse of their people, they lack the vision and the leadership style to serve and lead, they are the curse of enlightenment because they seek being a follower and loyal only to his president or king regardless of what he can do, he doesn't care all what he cares for is power and money.

Obviously a vacuum has been created in all Arab countries, Political, economic and social vacuum and that vacuum has been filled by the ruthless concept of Wahhabism covered by the umbrella of religion which is the only entity that can unify the Arab masses, so enlightenment stand no chance to revolve for the weakness of the elite and educated, and the presence of political, economic and social vacuum that enhanced poverty and increased the gap between rich and poor, coupled with economic recession and increased unemployment, all these changes, events were the proper medium to grow radicalism that paved the way to terrorism, so when we fight terrorism we need to fight the concept through improving and modernizing education and religion in schools building a generation that is Enlightened not a generation of followers and blind submissive to religion clergy.

Wahhabism has erased the Egyptian open mentality through its overwhelming financial support in building religion institutes that adopt their sick methodology and propagate radicalism, also they produced a whole generation of haters and killers brainwashed under the influence of religion clergy who filled their pockets with money coming from different sources and we all know about that.

So we need to combat terrorism not terrorist through, education, knowledge, freedom and compassion this is the only solution, not guns, grenades, rockets and fighter planes, those weapons didn't eliminate ISIS and probably it wont because the Terrorist production source is active.

We need to set the progressive thinkers, free from prisons, allow enlightenment, respect our moral values, promote unconditional love, disperse tolerance and enhance wellbeing, how could be a law exists that throw those who question religion explanation into prison under the umbrella that they are non believers and infidels they are not they doing their utmost efforts in questioning, debating and reflecting on aspects of religion explanation that is totally out of touch.

Those free thinkers in Egypt has been locked out under the false claim that they insulted Islam which is a false accusation, they are questioning the people who are explaining Islam and that was considered sin what an absurd uncivilized approach,

Egypt now is experiencing Schizophrenia as the Authority claims for enlightenment and renewing and reinventing religion preaching but on the contrast, it still follows the law that imprison people for questioning the religion explanation, what a contradiction that should come to an end otherwise our Egypt will be wasted by religion conflicts

We tend to forget that happiness doesn't come as a result of getting something we don't have, but of appreciating what we do have.

Chapter 11

Leadership

Leadership is not about title or position or power it is about Action and Example

I have been intrigued by the topic of leadership in my classes and I was privileged in several occasions to address this topic from my prospective marinated with my passion and experience.

I have studied and digested plenty of leadership quotes and I used them as my personal reference in my life Journey triggering and stimulating my approach and style in teaching the concept of leadership, one of the great books that I ever read is Robin Sharma leader who has no title and there is an abundance of great books that can change your life in the field of leadership,

A leader derives his strength and inspiration from having an acute and irreversible lust for learning. A fire in the belly to become relentless amid naysayers. The ability to spot the finest in people and to fan their flames of excellence. Having and executing beautiful goals + dreams., owns an uncommon adherence to politeness, punctuality and graciousness., posses A heroic devotion to standing in full expression of creativity + originality, thrives to be A breathtaking desire to become the undisputed heavyweight champion of their craft., has No need to be like everyone else, demonstrate his No capability to convert pain into strength and heartbreak into joy and bliss.

A leader posses massive amount of energy that ignite his inspiration, rejects a stagnate situation or cling to the status quo, with his tremendous desire to enlighten many he become a devoted world builder, a game changer and a master

The path of mastery is not for the meek. The highway to audacity is not for the faint of heart. The route to world-class is a messy, chaotic, gorgeous, terrifying, fulfilling, brilliant, confusing ride. Not easy. But easy is vastly overrated

The credit for all acts of genius and mastery does go to the one in the arena. The one with the guts to hear the haters and keep moving ahead. The one who takes the leap and ends up bruised, battered and even bloodied. The one who hears the noisy voices of self-doubt yet trusts something larger and wiser within that encourages him to continue, against all odds.

Learn, Serve and inspire, for that's where growth lives. And that's where our greatest rewards lie. I want to be totally spent by the time I'm done. No point in dying with your gifts still within you.

A leader works to be inspired and focus on solutions not the problems

A Leader delivers results, adores perfection install his discipline and rituals and remain relentless till he delivers.

Leader embrace adversities, by welcoming the process as a gift not waiting for the final result, he believes in his compelling cause, deploy leadership performance and attitudes, he lives with devotion commitment and conviction to make his dreams comes true

Success has less to do with hard work and more to do with massive focus on your few best opportunities.

Why resist change when it's the main source of your growth?

The more you invest in growing and developing your mindset and way of seeing the world, the more everything you touch transforms in a breathtakingly positive way.

Pursuing perfection really does matter (in a world highly accepting of mediocrity).

Spending full days with zero technology to refuel or do important work is a game-changer.

Doing something super-nice for at least one stranger a day gives them a gift and an even larger one to yourself.

Adore your parents. You'll miss them when they're gone.

The smartest thing you can do to grow a great company is to first sweat getting A-players only onto your team and then sweat training and developing them so they play their A-game.

Have the discipline to clean out all the energy-draining people in your life. You really do rise or fall to the level of your associations.

Doing huge dreams, we have never done can be frightening. Yet when we push to the edges of our limits, our limits expand.

If you don't make the time for yourself to get inspired, no one around you will ever be inspired.

Your diet affects your moods. Eat like a superstar.

Talk less. Do more.

Integrity is more valuable than income.

Learn to love yourself. It's the great rule for being loving with other people.

When your dominant business focus is to deliver outrageous amounts of value to your customer's every time they do business with you, they become fanatical followers who tell the world about what you do.

Real leaders have the guts to have the hard conversations.

Your environment (your home, your office, the magazines you read etc.) dramatically affects your levels of achievement.

The quality of your practice affects the caliber of your performance.

Reviewing your Big 5 annual goals every morning and working on your plan every day is an exceptionally powerful way to breed unbeatable focus and drive.

Measure your success via your influence and impact versus only by your income and net worth.

To become successful, first learn how to be happy. Too many think that the route to happiness is to get successful. Untrue.

Getting ultra-fit lifts every other area of your life.

Self-belief is so incredibly important. Because if you don't believe you can achieve a vision/goal, then you won't even start to do the work needed to achieve that vision/goal.

Our biggest enemy is our own self-doubt. We really can achieve *extraordinary* things in our lives. But we sabotage our greatness because of our fear.

Smile It truly makes a difference to the people around you.
Just because excellent manners are not so common doesn't mean that excellent manners are not incredibly important.

Always remember that there's food on your table thanks to the customers you are privileged to serve.

It's so much better to fail trying than to not even get into the game.

Music just makes life a whole lot better.

You can change the world or you can worry about fitting in but you just can't do both.

Change is hard at first, messy in the middle and beautiful at the end.

The real key to getting great things done is stop doing so many good things.

Small little details done excellently and consistently stack up into something the world sees as Mastery.

Spend time in nature to renew and refuel.

Less entertainment, more education.

Gratitude is the antidote to misery.

We become happier not by accumulating more things but by creating richer experiences.

Your self-identity is what really determines your income, influence, impact and lifestyle. Retrain that and your bigness comes out to play.

The more you serve, the more joyful you'll become.

Life's short. Have fun.

-

I would love to share with you the leadership tips that inspire me

- Dream Big. Start small. Act now.
- . Victims make excuses. Leaders deliver results.
- . Clarity breeds mastery.
- Education is inoculation against disruption.

- A problem is only a problem when viewed as a problem.
- All change is hard at first, messy in the middle and gorgeous at the end.
- If you're not scared a lot you're not doing very much.
- Where victims see adversity, extreme achievers see opportunity.
- The project you are most resisting carries your greatest growth.
- . Small daily improvements over time lead to stunning results.
- Criticism is the price of ambition.
- Potential unexpressed turns to pain.
- Ordinary people love entertainment. Extraordinary people adore education.
- Your daily behavior reveals your deepest beliefs.
- . The only failure is not trying.
- Focus is more valuable than IQ.
- . To double your income, triple your investment in self-development.
- Your excuses are nothing more than the lies your fears have sold you.
- An addiction to distraction is the end of your creative production.
- Life is short. Be useful and enjoy it

Lift people up vs. tear others down., Use the words of leadership vs. the language of victimhood, take your health Don't worry about getting the credit for getting things done, Become part of the solution rather than part of the problem

Commit to mastery of your craft instead of accepting mediocrity in your work. Associate with people whose lives you want to be living.

Double your learning and you'll triple your success. Do something small yet scary every single day, Focus on people's strengths vs. obsessing around their weaknesses

Lead Without a Title. Say "please" and "thank you". Love your loved ones.

Do work that matters Smile more. And Listen more.

Chapter 12

Your best work

Do your best work by challenging the way you did things yesterday. Do your best work by allowing your passion to see the light of day.

Do your best work by becoming part of the solution versus growing the problem.

Do your best work by expecting nothing less than you playing at world-class. Do your best work by giving away the credit (especially when you crave it) Do your best work by practicing your skills so you become a master in your craft and domain.

Do your best work by releasing excuses and doing important things. Do your best work by getting up when you've been knocked down. Do your best work by keeping your promises; to others and to yourself.

Do your best work by showing integrity?

Do your best work by delivering more value than anyone could ever expect from you. Do your best work by making time to refill your well.

Do your best work by having a strong foundation at home. Do your best work by becoming as fit as a pro athlete. Do your best work by doing work that makes a difference and inspires others to do the same -

You are not just paid to work. You are paid to be uncomfortable – and to pursue projects that scare you.

Take care of your relationships and the money will take care of itself.

You can't help others reach for their highest potential until you're in the process of reaching for yours.

While victims condemn change, leaders grow inspired by change. Small daily improvements over time create stunning results. Surround yourself with people courageous enough to speak truthfully about what's best for your organization and the customers you serve.

. Every moment in your life should be a moment of truth (to either show you live by the values you profess – or you don't). Copying what your competitors is doing just leads to being second best. Become obsessed with the user experience such that every touch point of doing business with you leaves people speechless. No, breathless. If you're in business, you're in show business. The moment you get to work, you're on stage. Give us the performance of your life. Be a Master of Your Craft. And practice + practice + practice.

Read magazines you don't usually read. Talk to people who you don't usually speak to. Go to places you don't commonly visit. Disrupt your thinking so it stays fresh, hungry, and brilliant. Remember that what makes a great business – in part – are the seemingly insignificant details. Obsess over them. Good enough just isn't good enough. Brilliant things happen when you go the extra mile for every single customer. An addiction to distraction is the death of creative production. Enough said. If you're not failing regularly, you're definitely not making much progress. Lift your teammates up versus tear your teammates down. Anyone can be a critic. What takes guts is to see the best in people. Remember that a critic is a dreamer gone scared. Leadership's no longer about position. Now, it's about passion. And having an impact through the genius-level work that you do. The bigger the dream, the more important the team. If you're not thinking for yourself, you're following – not leading. Work hard. But build an exceptional family life. What's the point of reaching the mountaintop but getting there alone? The job of the leader is to develop more leaders. The antidote to deep change is daily learning. Investing in your professional and personal development is the smartest investment you can make. Period. Smile. It makes a difference. Say "please" and "thank you". It makes a difference. Shift from doing mindless toil to doing valuable work. Remember that a job is only just a job if all you see it as is a job. Don't do your best work for the applause it generates but for the personal pride it delivers. The only standard worth reaching for is BIW (Best in World). In the new world of business, everyone works in Human Resources. In the new world of business, everyone's part of the leadership team. Words can inspire. And words can destroy. Choose yours well. You become your excuses. You'll get your game-changing ideas away from the office versus in the middle of work. Make time for solitude. Creativity needs the space to present itself. The people who gossip about others when they are not around are the people who will gossip about you when you're not around. It could take you 30 years to build a great reputation and 30 seconds of bad judgment to lose it. The client is always watching. The way you do one thing defines the way you'll do everything. Every act matters. To be radically optimistic isn't soft. It's hard. Crankiness is easy. People want to be inspired to pursue a vision. It's your job to give it to them. Every visionary was initially called crazy.

The purpose of work is to help people. The other rewards are inevitable by-products of this singular focus. Remember that the things that get scheduled are the things that get done. Keep promises and be impeccable with your word. People buy more than just your products and services. They invest in your credibility.

So to perform at your best not only in work but in life, you need to be prepared mentally, physically and emotionally, establish the mind set of possibilities potentials and opportunities, never be scared from change, say yes to what scare you that will release your hidden gifts that will Awe you, and always be obsessed with serving and giving.

Genius resides in simplicity. And simplicity is perfection so Trust yourself and create space for your creative talent to flow.

Chapter 13

A prospective of
A hero after 5 years

5 years' ado a famous video was shown, which did not only ease the grief of the father of a dead son but eased on all Bahrainis the effect of a new phase in which Bahrain experienced painful events in 2011.

"The father of a Bahraini and a very honorable Egyptian doctor" was the title of the video clip which showed a consultant emergency physician Alaa Zidan at "Sitra Health Centre" holding the hand of the father embracing and kissing him, and asking him and others to stop thanking him "Do not say so, do not say so, this is my duty, I am one of you, my wife is Bahraini, she also has come with me to help you…"

Doctor Alaa Zidan was the soother, he was that difference in everything that happened that day, he is a Bahraini Egyptian epitome for "medical neutrality", he did not escape, did not lie or switch off his phone, says one of the doctors.

"I am Sitra's champion, because I treated people with love," says Dr. Zidan

"I am a liberal and I hate politics. An Egyptian who likes to work in Bahrain, worked and still working here for 18 years, and I am proud to treat patients regardless of their religion, nationality, or color."

"The father of the dead Bahraini changed my life; it was a hug that involved compassion, love and peace". Dr. Zidan was on sick leave on "Sitra's Incident" day, but a group of doctors contacted him because they needed his leadership in dealing with patients at Sitra Health Centre; "I was called while I was sick, But I didn't hesitate a moment to work for Bahrain."

Zidan, the Egyptian doctor lover of Bahrain, worked in a tough atmosphere to treat injured Bahrainis,

The health center was not safe due to the riots but Zidan stayed put "I was working for more than 10 hours, and led a great team of my colleagues, and my young students, I really liked that work,"

"It was a difficult and cruel experience, but proved that compassion has no nationality," says Dr. Zidan; it was the most moving experience that change his life and inspired him to spread the message of saving people's lives, "I cannot forget the day that changed my life."

Zidan became after this incident, a well known worldwide speaker about "love and attachment to spiritual values" and an international professor known in "saving people's lives and promoting unconditional love."

"Politics and religion for me is love and peace", via "Twitter"; Doctor Alaa Zidan tweeted @coolzidan for more than Four years, about love, mercy, compassion, and all the noble meanings related to humanity.

All his tweets had the #Bahrain "I never felt that I am not Bahraini," He talks a lot about his detained fellow doctors "who put their lives on the line for patients," he emotionally expresses his great pride of this experience, talking about his passion for Bahrain, and his passion for Sitra, "when my life ends, please burry me in Sitra."

Zidan Says "when you are the doctor who had seen everything in Sitra, those scenes would remain haunting your dreams" and adds, "I miss my patients, my friends, my brothers and sisters in Sitra. That simplicity, kindness and warm welcoming, but I feel like I'm with them, my soul never left Sitra because the power of love cannot be defeated, and no one can stop me from loving Bahrain."

Zidan travels between Florida and Bahrain, diligently to per sue his mission in saving lives

I look to this experience and I learn from it every day, the best lesson is never bother about how people think of you, what is important is how you think of yourself, also love and compassion always prevails no matter what are the consequences, and fear is an elusion once you conquer Fear nothing will constrain your ability nor imprison your sense of giving.

Another lesson that I learned from this experience is that we are all one, units interconnected in this wonderful amazing miraculous universal fabric.

I have elaborated more in my previous book "My Own Reflections" about The events that took place in Bahrain on 2011, and approached it objectively with no political nor religion inclination to any side, my approach was simply human as a doctor who saves live, relieves pain and bring joy to his patients

I don't claim any personal glory, nor any gain whatsoever, what has been done by me is one of plenty of success stories that happened in Bahrain and around the World.

I will never stand in shadows I am here to make waves of love and compassion. that is who I am.

Chapter 14

Science and religion
Friends or enemies

I believe that not because I can't see or feel something doesn't mean it doesn't exist

But I am not with blind submission and undisputed following to religion doctrine explained by certain clergy prospective who owns a certain focused agenda of labelling and separation, Ernest Hemingway once stated that all thinking men are Atheists what can you elicit from this quote is that science and religion are rivals they hate each other, as if they are in a contest were there is desperation of win on the expense of our moral values., We a lot of scientist around the globe who are a true believers defeating the idea that a true scientist cant be a believer.

There are several ways where science and religion would be friends as science refer to the domain of knowledge and Religion refer to the domain of Faith, they can be separate in the sense that Religion Explains the ultimate reason and the real truth of life, while science verify, test and elaborate objectively how to reach the truth

I believe that science and religion coexist with a strong bond that should encourage more freedom, debate, questioning and inquiry

Having both leading a complete separate and independent domain of inquiry can be extremely difficult and cumbersome, because not all the truth can be tested and examined through a proper scientific methodology, can we confirm or deny a historical event that took place by scientific method that comprises the pillars of scientific thinking, posing a question, leading to a hypothesis, applying testing and reaching a conclusion that needs to be retested and reconfirmed before being an absolute fact

There are other examples of truths that cannot be adequately tested via the scientific method, such as the laws of logic (science presupposes logic), the actual existence of other minds, or other metaphysical truths. Yet we all believe logic, the existence of other minds, and many other such truths exist. In addition, we all believe in many experiential truths like love which no scientific experiment can demonstrate or capture in a test tube.

We seem to have been led to the conclusion that there are certain places which science and religion overlap, but others in which they do not. This is the third view of the relationship between science and religion.

Albert Einstein once said that "A legitimate conflict between science and religion cannot exist. Science without religion is lame, religion without science is blind." Although Einstein did not believe in a "personal" God (he was a deist) he was right when he said that true religion and accurate science cannot be in disharmony with one-another in the areas in which they overlap.

How religion differs from science

An objection that may come to mind at this point. "But science is different. Science gives us facts; religion just gives us opinions. Religion doesn't lead to certainty."

While it is true that science often leads to facts (keeping in mind that current scientific truths are often later corrected by further research) we should keep in mind that **most of the truths we believe are based on probability, not absolute certainty**. Even most of the scientific facts we believe are based on what we've been told. Most of us have not personally conducted experiments to prove that gravity exists, but we believe it to be true.

One thing that makes evaluating religious beliefs particularly difficult is that they are multifaceted. Religion addresses not just empirical truths (though these are very important), but also addresses experiential, emotional, moral, and metaphysical truths.

We have the reason to believe that science and faith are not, in fact, enemies. They both attempt to elaborate, describe and focus upon reality, sometimes in complimentary ways, other times in ways that only their particular methodology can do.

For some, scientific study can lead them away from their faith, as their erroneous understanding of real faith conflicts with their new scientific knowledge. Others, however, are led to faith through studying science. He tells his story in the article My Search for Truth. the truth that we are searching for, is the truth that truly satisfies our multifaceted search for intimacy, meaning, and destiny.

I am more inclined that spirituality is a strong bond and a brilliant link that connects religion and science.

Science can not discredit religion, nor religion can discredit science they are the sides of the same coin and the coin is the universe and existence.

Spirituality is the key and the link that will bring religion and science together, in order to erase ignorance, hatred, violence and terrorism.

Accepting and respecting and tolerating other people beliefs and religions, let our differences fade by remembering the fact that we are all one, no one among us is superior, we are strings connected in this beautiful universal symphony.

Let's be open and accepting to others people opinions and views without marking or labelling them as outlaws, lets unlock the mentality of free thinking, welcome and embrace and learn from our differences, lets stop victimization and move forward to serve and make a difference.

I believe that the issue of religion and science being at cross roads is of utmost significance in further igniting sectorial conflicts and wars around the globe, it is a matter of extreme priority for all of us, unless we tackle, deal and approach this issue the world will be heading towards chaos and disasters.

We should invest on human wellbeing, community development, improving education and revamping health services, to build a tolerant, lovable, compassionate, and grateful generation.

We should build leaders who spare no effort in establishing a vision of peace, abundance and prosperity, we should discourage frank and blind submission, disregarding our critical and free thinking to explore and learn the truth.

We should direct our attention to our children encouraging them to think, challenge and debate instead of turning them into a blind follower like a flock of sheep.

We should bridge the gap between rich and poor, make nature part of our life, empower entrepreneurship, Re-Imagine Education and Nurture Health.

Chapter 15

From Florida with love

For the past 7 years I have been travelling to Orlando maybe three times a year with my fun companion, my lovely partner, the love of my life, my wife Hala, visiting my only sister Naglaa, so after the events of Arab spring my life has been split between Bahrain and Orlando and luckily enough there are a lot of similarity between them

The weather is more or less similar except for the showers in Orlando and humidity is less

But the spirit of simplicity prevails in both places, simple, joyful and adorable people around you, the only difference is the size and vastness of Orlando compared to Bahrain.

Florida changed my life, empowered me to change my perspective when I become more close in my relationship with my both sisters who truly supported me in my adversities and empowered me by believing in what I do without Judgment, I was always thrilled to see my son and daughter in law several time a year till 2013, when suddenly my Brother in law took his kids and moved to another state, so we were family of 6 turned and reduced to a family of 3,

Myself, my Wife and My young sister Naglaa this dramatic and swift change took place after the Death of my older sister November 2013, Just one Month later her kids were taken by their father to another state.

Our whole life changed up side down, because the kids were far away from us and we could not communicate with them as their father for one reason or another prevent that

Fulfilling a certain agenda that I refrain from discussing it because it is beyond the scope of this book, these kids My son and daughter in law were the joy of our lives and became more attached to me after their mam death, and suddenly they vanished out of our life, which was a serious blow to My young sister who raised them both, so you could imagine the intense stress that my sister was subjected to.

Naglaa survived this serious blow and over the past 2 years she demonstrated her agility, flexibility and accepted the current situation and she is working hard on herself with my support to move forward with her life.

Naglaa was relieved from her duties as a care giver to her both in laws and rejoiced her freedom, by having the time to look after herself, travel with us around the globe and she went with us several times to our favorite sanitary Thailand

Every thing always happens for a good Reason, I look to my sister now and I sense freedom instead of being a submissive servant and an ATM Machine to her in laws, she loves her self, take care of herself as for all her life she was only dedicated to her in laws, her in laws literally were her life.

This Story has a beginning but the end didn't come yet, but this is not important in the sense that we should believe that, life is about change, we are scared from change, fear the rebellion on our comfort zone disregarding the only fact in life which is change is inevitable and we should accept and live with it then we will be able to discover what we could have missed and that is the journey of happiness, because happiness is never a target happiness is a byproduct and the essence of happiness lies in the process.

We are lucky to have my sister visiting us frequently in Bahrain and she became one of Bahrain lovers.

The quest of adapting to any change in your life is painful at the beginning but it is magical at the end, because it open doors of opportunities and always make us think out of the box.

Chapter 16

New Job

Welcoming risks has been always part of my personality, believing that taking risks and doing the things that scares you makes you joyful and happy, you discover your hidden gifts and missed potentials,

Following the Arab spring I changed my career and perused my true passion which is serving people through teaching and promoting the sacred message of unconditional love and saving lives.

I have been teaching in the medical school for the past 13 years and till present in Bahrain as a part timer and that job brought joy in my life by helping, teaching and supporting my students who are the future health care providers in Bahrain.

The missing issue was that my life turned to be riskless, stale and routine, I was entrapped in monotonicity and stagnation.

I was under the seduction of the safety of comfort zone to the extent that I couldn't part with it and that was the true danger facing me curtailing my creativity and paralyzing my innovation, I was paralyzed by fear, immediately I acknowledged the problem and I decided to conquer my fear by taking risks

I couldn't surrender to what is obvious enemy which is fear, I couldn't let go of fear eating me up, I couldn't let the comfort zone and stagnation posses my life,

We create our own reality and we are all destined to greatness, if we neglect this fact this means that we are non believers in the divine that created us to enjoy, serve, love and make a difference, if I surrender to the seduction of comfort zone, I will be a hippo crate who is not practicing what he preaches, I will be nothing but darkness a serpent who poisons all who comes around him. They inspired, empowered me in several occasions and I earned amazing feedbacks from my students and great testimonials as well.

My full time job during the past 4 years added to teaching in the university was being a consultant in health and safety teaching the domain of health and safety in one of the well known private training institutes in Bahrain, it was a fulfilling job, I learned a lot boosted my reputation as one of the well known trainers in the field of Health and safety and Emergency care, I have been recognized by a lot of international accreditation bodies and earned 3 honorary Ph.Ds.

Earning titles, positions acknowledgments and accomplishments is a good thing definitely it reflects your presence and galvanize more opportunities because, I invested in my self development and education.

There is a time were I felt well established in my job, doing extremely well, success has been my company all the time when I was working in this institute, but something was missing it is the thing that awe you, pumps your heart and open your eyes, I turned into a robot who knows his craftsmanship by hard and do everything automatically and subconsciously due to my deliberate practice that led me to mastery in teaching, but again I was missing something, kept searching for this missing thing but I couldn't find it.

My stagnation and surrender to the comfort zone didn't last long and then I was blessed by my new Job that represent a true challenge which is heading training and creative development in the whole GCC, Middle East and Asia in one of the most well known and prestigious corporation around the globe, working to make things happen

I Joined a dream team a brilliant family destined to serve, excel and evolve.

We developed our corporate culture that revolves around the core value, of perfection, freedom, creativity, quality and love.

So my dream came through, I asked, I believed and I received.

Chapter 17

The defeat of a nasty Disease

November 2013, I was subjected to one of the severest blows in my life the death of my beloved old sister Safaa, I remember quiet well when my young Sister Naglaa Called to inform me with this bad news.

When I visited her grave in the suburbs of Orlando Florida its was raining heavily, but I Kept sitting in front of her grave and I visualized meeting her and we had a beautiful dialogue telling me "Alaa why you are so sad and crying, my body left but my soul is with you and I know how much my kids love you, my brother you are my ball of light who inspired me, you are my Hero who stood fearless for what you truly believe, you are, you are the voice of the voiceless, you are my healer"

That was what she told me, few hours later I collapsed and I was Transferred to Orlando medical center where I was exposed to a battery of endless investigations that revealed that I was perfectly normal, I believe that what I have exposed to was a near death experience emerging from my sincere intention to meet my sister who passed away but she is deep seated in my heart.

One month following the death of my sister, I was sitting in my sanctuary (My office), and my wife spotted a big spot in my head with no hair, within one week from my wife observation I LOST all my Hair, my head was looking like a chess board and even I could see by mirror some nice drawings in my head like someone riding a horse,

I developed an aggressive disease called Alopecia Areiata, losing my hair on my scalp, eyebrows and nostrils this is a disease that comes to people who have very high immunity to the extent that theses immune cells can fight the healthy cells, this aggressive disease developed because of the tremendous grief and stress that resulted from death of my sister.

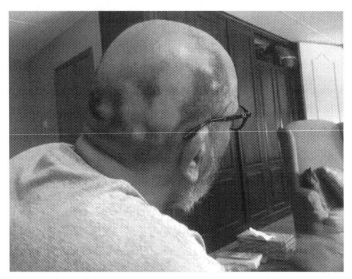

A chess board at my Scalp

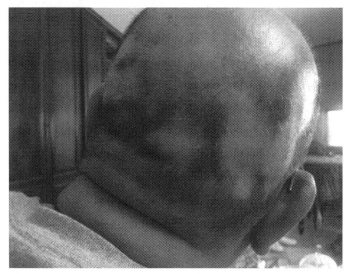

The disease that I defeated

The were no response to the medical treatment given to me, but I never felt down, I just let go and lived my life reflecting on the disease that attacked me, I started reframing the situation and thinking positively, This Disease attack intelligent people with powerful immunity, so I looked to the whole predicament from a positive prospective that I am intelligent, sensitive and my immunity is superb!!

Over more than sixteen months, my journey with Alopecia, I learned the Art of letting go, acceptance and gratitude, I excelled in my work, developed creative courses touches behavior and attitude which inspired my students and I earned amazing testimonials from my students and experts.

I am obsessed with serving people, my fuel, oxygen and fire is help, support and serve., I believe that we should follow our heart our passion reveal our genius provide unconditional love and project joy.

I will never let the hero in myself perish, I will only fail if I stop trying, probably every week I enroll in a course that cover a domain that I have no clue about it, because investing in your education is the key to make a difference, it unwinds your creativity and embraces fear and challenges, formal education makes a living, but self education makes the sky your only limit.

The disease made me a warrior of light, I am a warrior of light a lion not a sheep a victor but not a victim a leader without a title but not a follower

The disease helped me to unlock my charisma, evolved my self –belief to trigger my spectacular achievements, I was able to ignite my passion because I found my purpose which is serve, serve and serve.

Happy to defeat this disease with the spectacular support of my wife, my sister, my family, my friends and my students, I believe without their support I would be buried in the grave of Darkness, negativity and Depression.

I would like to convey my deepest gratitude for being blessed with adversities and setbacks that polished my ability, empowered my creativity and unlocked my potentials and leashed my passion, and I couldn't forget how my family stood beside me and the great American dermatologist who treated me and turned to love my spiritual and positive attitude.

When I fully recovered I thought what could be better than giving her the art of happiness book by the Dali lama as a token of thankfulness and gratitude and she was so happy and told me that her daughter loved the book and she is involved in a lot of charity activities as philanthropist.

Chapter 18

Hope

Hope is all what we have, we can not live without hope, Life has no fragrance, nor taste without hope, there is no meaning for life, hope is all what we got and it can change your perception in situations that can be beyond your scope of coping.

We are not meant to be suffering, even if we are subjected to adversities we are created with protective gifts, and proactive options to deal with difficulties, but I believe that hope is a good starting point where you can build an established foundation to hardwire your mind to be positive, positivity, compassion, unconditional love, gratitude, thankfulness, mindfulness, purpose, vision and over and above a clear meaningful intention to serve and give.

Our common mistakes is we give up so soon, without realizing that we can learn and overturn a setback into a success story.

We are meant to love and be loved, we are meant to excel and use our genuis

We are meant to be compassionate not cruel, we are meant to be creative and courageous, because we are the creatures of the divine who urge us to use our gifts we are gifted creatures that is our very basic structure.

The things that irritate and annoy and anger you are entry points into your evolution and elevation as a human being. They are signposts for what you need to work on and the fears you need to face. They are gifts of growth. You can blame the people who trigger you and make it all about them. Or you can do the courageous thing and look deeply into yourself to discover the reason for your negative reaction. The fears you don't own become your prison bars.

And as you begin to shed light on your personal weaknesses and take responsibility for them, you actually begin the process of shedding them. You become stronger. More powerful. More of who you were meant to be.

Problems are servants. They help you grow and lead to better things, both within your organization and in your life. To resist them is to avoid growth and progress. Embrace and get the best from the challenges in front of you. And understand that the only people with no problems are dead.

An unhappy customer yelling at you might seem like a problem. But to a person thinking like a leader, that scenario is also an opportunity to improve the organization's processes to ensure that doesn't happen again. So the problem has actually helped to improve the company.

An interpersonal conflict at work can seem like a problem. But if you think like a leader and use the circumstance to build understanding, promote communication and enrich the relationship, the problem has actually made you better. It has been fodder for your growth and served you nicely.

An illness or a divorce or the loss of a loved one might seem like a problem. Sure it's painful (been there, done that). But I've been shaped by my saddest experiences. They've brought me depth, compassion and wisdom. They've made me the man that I am. I wouldn't trade them for the world.

Problems reveal genius. World-class organizations have a culture that sees problems as opportunities for improvement. A mistake is only a mistake if you make it twice. And world-class human beings use their stumbling blocks as stepping stones. They use their failures to bring them closer to success. They don't see problems. They see possibilities. And that's what makes them great.

Think people are good and you walk through your days with an open heart. And that behavior actually becomes your reality because people do good things for good people. Think you deserve the best and your actions will reflect that confidence. Better actions will then drive better results.

Expect to be one of the great ones in your career or within your country. That brilliant thinking shapes the way you work and the way you show up in general. And that world-class conduct presents world-class outcomes. And the core of such an attitude and action is having hope and the deepest commitment to believe in your true self.

Life can be hard. We all have our good seasons as well as our difficult ones. But hard times bring many blessings. Like strength of character, self-knowledge, courage, greater understanding and deeper compassion. Some of the qualities of the very best leaders that have walked before us.

We grow the most as human beings during our roughest times. So why do we judge them as bad – when they bring such good? The challenging pieces of our lives just might be when we are most alive. And they always bring tiny miracles. If you are awake to them. And you are immersed in the ocean of Hope.

Chapter 19

Fear and conspiracy theory

Every day, probably you hear about conspiracy theory, in the international media I believe it became a culture among us, I am not defying the concept of conspiracy theory and it was found to be the trigger of several disasters and crises and I wont discuss it because it is beyond the scope of this book.

The media orchestrated its mighty power to control the mind of the masses by perpetuating the concept of conspiracy theory to the extent that it became embedded and deeply established in our cultures. To the extent that every setback is explained and justified due to conspiracy theory

Conspiracy theory has and remains to be used continuously by governments for several reasons, is to justify their setbacks in not meeting people expectations and the use of excessive force and iron fist aiming for securing their power.

Conspiracy theory is one of the main tools that inject, develop and raise fear in the hearts of people till it becomes a monster that control and manipulate the masses and converting them into followers like a flock of sheep.

Conspiracy theory to my mind in most of the situations of my life I truly believe that they are like a bogyman a paper monster that has no existence and not even worth a flicker of a second thinking about it, when I embraced my fears, I enjoyed and excelled in most the aspects of my life.

Let me tell you a story, after the end of my career as a doctor, my friends kept telling me

> **"Why did you involve yourself in saving lives, during the Events that took place, March 2011 in Bahrain did you see what happened, you lost your job and you will be kicked out of the country, why you involve yourself, you were already having a sick leave, you risked your life you were going to die, why should you do that, we know very well that you are a competent doctor, but your job is to be a follower, now see what happened to you, you are jobless and penniless and you have been labelled as a traitor and you and your whole family cursed you haven't seen what is written about you in social media and newspapers shame on you"**

Those who I thought that they are my fiends they even avoided seeing or answering my calls

Imagine I am talking about people who I knew for more than 10 years, but to be honest, I thank and send love to those who, avoided, tarnished, insulted and attacked me and I never hold any grudge against them

Every thing happens for a good reason with the support of Allah, My wife, My two sisters, My students my wife family and very few friends and over and above the people of Bahrain, I became a Hero

They are calling me nicknames like the honorable Egyptian doctor, I became well known all around Bahrain and outside Bahrain as well, I was converted into a symbol of tolerance, love and peace

I am such a lucky that any where I go I am well known and opportunities are opened, and when I accidently those who humiliated and avoided and left me to sink in the trench of darkness, they come so fast to hug me telling me we are so happy to see you and we are so sorry that we didn't support you, and My answer is

> **"Please never apologize you are my friend, I do understand what has been done and never worry about me, I truly love you and I am thankful to you," these words come from my heart and I truly mean it, I never live in the past because I always honor the present moment.**

Fear paralyze you and if you read the history you will find that if any country is led by fear, oppression, imprisonment of creative thinking, silencing the voices of reason, and force then such countries will crumble and erased.

Fear is the obstacle of prosperity and progress, countries progress by Freedom., creativity, science and true religion, countries prosper through fulfilling their true values love, compassion, dedication determination and hard work

Fear controls and enslaves those who are seduced by the safety of the comfort zone, who resist change.

The mighty Media plays a pivotal role in spreading fears and investing on people misery and people falls in the trap and they are lost in the web of darkness.

Fear deprives your creativity, inhibits your imagination and curtail your gifts, we should be aware that we are born gifted, we are born genius and we are born with love and compassion imprinted in our DNA, when we surrender to our fears we become so distant from believing in God who created us with all these infinite gifts at the first place.

It is obvious to every one that the conventional struggle between Religion Institute and Science and I am precise when I mean religion Institute not the religion, because the true religion whatever is Islam, Christianity, Judaism, Buddhism etc. is always a source of enlightenment, this struggle remains and is increasing tremendously and the gap is widening, and the Atheist created a military faction called militant atheist who are seizing the opportunity to insult religion and God under the umbrella of spirituality, they forgot that spirituality is the brilliant link between Science and Religion.

One of useless irrational argument of Atheist is that god didn't create the universe and that the Universe was created by the Big Bang theory again but who banged the bang it is the source, the creator, the divine intelligence ALLAH.

Another argument by atheists is the victimization and conspiracy theory, by claiming that they are mistreated and labelled as forsaken outsiders and they have no moral values.

Again that might be right in some communities, but to me and my view is that I never judge, nor label anyone the issue of belief and Religion is a personal Relation between the person and his god that he believe in, I have no right to label. Compare or judge anyone the minute that I do that this means that I inaugurated my self as an irrevocable trustee on him, that is truly unacceptable, we should not invade people freedom to think, but that doesn't mean I wont defend and stand fearlessly for what I believe without anger nor hatred but with open mind.

This struggle takes different form at a state and organizational level when you find struggle between a closed, aging, wrinkled, old fashioned and slow System and the Elite who are usually few and adopt reform, creativity, unorthodox progressive thinking and Enlightenment who apply reasoning, critical thinking and Science, such elite they are always crushed by the system because they are few and they give up early.

The opportunists invest on such struggle and they rise to the top of the system in different areas, eventually they gain power and start to eliminate any opposition establishing Iron fist system, depriving Freedom and Democracy and once Freedom and Democracy is absent then the system collapses and that what we learned from history.

I was about to fall in the trap of grudge and hatred, when we were against Muslim brotherhood when they ran Egypt and after June 30 the liberals came to power and I was happy but within few days, the liberals turned into monsters of hate and preaches of vengeance against Muslim Brotherhood and the focus was on hating Muslim Brotherhood but not on rebuilding and reforming Egypt and that is a big mistake, because at the end we are all one we want our country to evolve.

Power allures, and deceives, Power feeds the ego and create fear doubt, the true power is not control it is power of inspiration, imagination, love a, compassion, courage and creativity.

Progress in any country is generated by Freedom, Democracy and creativity and history is an evidence.

Chapter 20

A brief meeting with an Inspirational Person

Two years ago I was honored to moderate Technical sessions in Leadership and safety culture in one of the most prestigious National safety council Expo San Diego USA.

I had the pleasure during the conference activities to attend in a fully packed main hall to be among the audience of the last raw sitting beside the love of my life, a key note speech by my one of my inspirational persons whom I admire tremendously Dr. Scot Geller and he was talking about motivation for over one hour, I couldn't sit on my chair from the extent of how I was totally focused watching his body language and his passion

Amazing energy, joyful attitude, brilliant connection with his audience.

Few minutes prior the end of Dr. Scot speech, I was whispering to my wife telling her, "my intuition is telling me that I will meet this brilliant guy"

"My wife whispered back telling you can't the whole hall is packed how you will come in a tiny hall corridor from the last raw to the front stage to shake hands with him it is very difficult"

I told my wife I choose to do what my gut feeling telling me

Once the speech came to an end the whole audience ran to the front stage, I told My wife' just wait on your chair if you want and I ll meet you later ',

I walked very fast as if I am a sharp knife slicing fresh butter within few minutes I was in front of

Dr. Scot telling him well done, immediately he shacked my hand, he told me you are full of light and he gave me his personal green wrist band written on it **Actively caring people**. Which was the main theme of his speech, and till this very moment I wear this beautiful meaningful wrist band which is Dr. Scot personal one such an honor to remind me that I have to care, love and be compassionate.

You Ask, You Believe and You Receive.

Thank you Dr. Scot for inspiring me, supporting and giving me the honor to meet you.

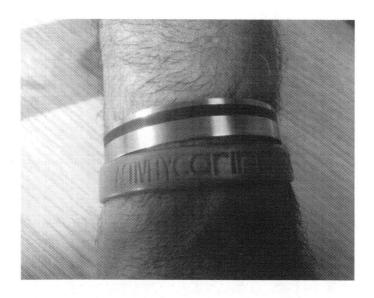

My Actively caring people wrist band given to me by Prof. Dr.
Scot Geller

Chapter 21

The End

The Message

Writing this book brings joy in my life and, always generates a positive energy, journaling your days was the trigger that enabled me to have outstanding source of information which is daily journal which is plenty of pages and it is written in a chronological order, but I tried as much as I can to provide some thoughts, reflections and stories of my life after 2011 till 2015, I couldn't cover all stories for some of them haven't ended yet and I thought about writing the book about all my ideas, reflections and actions during 2011 till 2015 but not in chronological order, because I don't want to be calculative but I want to be intuitive, I want to follow my heart but not my mind, I want to feel flawing in the beautiful universal space dancing and grateful and thoughtful of his life and his mission with no propaganda nor personal glory.

My mission is to serve and help people to evolve and progress and to create a well cohesive universal community anchored with, openness, compassion, love and enlightenment, a community based on scientific critical thinking.

A community that thrives for freedom and Democracy, a community that has zero tolerance to religion discrimination, a community that encourages scientific thinking in religion narratives and explanation books.

I love telling my stories because there might be something that you can make use and learn from it, we have to learn from our mistakes, and convert these mistakes into opportunities.

I had no any intention to offend anyone that is not my style, I critique only for the better and I have nothing personal against anyone, it is your choice to agree or disagree with what I wrote.

I believe this book reflects some parts of my life, and I still ask myself did you explore all your dark boxes, I would say yes and it was such a joy to do that so that I can write about it and then the readers might not do it.

We need to free our selves from the fixed belief that happiness is the target the final destination the ultimate purpose, I believe that happiness is the journey, the trip and the process and the core joy lies in the process not the result.

I believe creating a civil society needs freedom and democracy, freedom of speech, innovation, enhancing creativity, encouraging reform, embracing change, erasing judgments, victimization. And comparison.

Full dedication to education and health reform, and that will unlock the chains of labelling each, according to religion, race, gender.

We can not create a civil society, while free progressive thinkers, are tortured and imprisoned and religion contempt law is implemented while it is unconstitutional.

A civil society can't be created in an environment deprived of open dialogue and freedom.

I believe that there is no discipline that you can't learn, there is no skill that you can't master

We have always to give more than we get, after all those years that I spent, I do my best to enjoy every given moment, to serve, sometimes I face setbacks, moments of defeats but any negative thoughts are very brief and probably unremarkable, and I keep on rolling, what is the point to brag and complain about something, Be the change, whatever scare me I consider it the starting point of discovering my true self.

I still have a lot to catch in this beautiful life which I chose to do, one day I will share my choices when they happen or in other words when my true intentions are translated into actions.

Everyone is vulnerable and can be exposed to difficulties, adversities and hurdles in life that can lead to a state of depression, despair and lack of self esteem, these difficulties can be the triggering point of two paths and it is your choice to pick one of them., either you surrender and accept the fact that you are a loser and this is just a false fact that dangles in your mind, haunts you, till it owns and control you. you become a slave with no heart, your will is broken and you remain a follower but never changer.

You might be rich, successful but you never discovered your true love, passion and purpose and paralyzed by fear.

Or you can choose the path of fearlessness, love and compassion, following your true self your inner self the gut feeling that guides you to what you are truly passionate about.

In my most major events in my life my decisions followed my heart my gut feeling, it might not look rational to my calculative mind or probably I had seen it, consciously irrational or risky.

The decision to let go of my sons to live with their mother was a difficult decision, my mind always tell me keep the kids let the mother go away, but my intuition tells me let the kids go with their mother, because I believe separating kids from their mother is far worse than separating them from their father, mothers are the backbone of any society, our generation needs dedicated mothers, so I erased my ego and it turns that I came to the proper decision, my kids are well and they are enjoying a nice life, although they are away but I would risk my joy for having them for the sake of their wellbeing.

The Decision of helping injured patients regardless of their gender, color, race and religion affiliation, was one of best decision that I risked my life and career and I never regret doing it, in fact if the time is rewind through a beautiful real time button, I would have done more

This decision carried my legacy as a simple honorable Egyptian doctor who stood for what he believes, and I will bring an important Dialogue between two of my best friends who were saying

> **"We ought to be proud that our friend not only a popular hero but he truly is passionate and a believer in what he does".**

Even if I took decisions that came to be extremely unsound or wrong, I never look back and I always move forward it is hurtful sometime and mind plays tricks on you showing how pathetic you are.

it takes a lot of guts and perseverance to overcome the false power of Ego supremacy.

I believe that positive energy, love and compassion will prevail, I believe that creativity, innovation and imagination will generate universal prosperity, accepting change and embracing fear are the road map to success and prosperity.

I now think about success, future goals and contribution to this world most of the time

Whenever I find myself indulging in negative thoughts patterns I consciously decide to focus on what is good and exciting, I know the first step in attaining success is being clear about what I want.

Happiness has never been a random event it is a step by step process of self realization of my own goals and the beauty is that I truly enjoy the ride.

My core message is

Behind me is infinite power, before me is endless possibility and around me is boundless opportunity

Challenges are what make life interesting. Overcoming them is what makes life meaningful.

Warriors of light

warrior of light is proud of his setbacks enjoys being himself because he know that no one can be better than himself except himself

A warrior of light is full of love, enjoys life, Adores & inspire people

A warrior of light never give up he loves his scares coz it reminds him how courageous he is

Warrior of light knows that before being Muslim Egyptian & doctor he knows that he should be Human

Warrior of light knows that before being Muslim Egyptian & doctor he knows that he should be Human

Warrior of light knows that before being Muslim Egyptian & doctor he knows that he should be Human

Warrior of light knows that before being Muslim Egyptian & doctor he knows that he should be Human

Warrior of light love forgive and enjoy he never judge nor compare

A warrior of light has no grudge against those who hurt him he loves them coz they unleashed his excellence

We tend to forget that happiness doesn't come as a result of getting something we don't have, but of appreciating what we do have.

I would love to share those beautiful words written by my sister in tribute to my late mother

"**Growing up as a child I used to stand so close to my mom in her shadow thinking that her grace will shine upon me as I went with her on my weekly trait for popcorn and ice cream I watched her feeding the homeless kids looking for sandwiches in the garbage bags, our home was open daily feeding the needy we shared the little food we had in our fridge with them as she sat them just like us on the same dinning table eating from the same plates we used same fork same spoon 25 plasters paper money brand new huge amount 40 years ago she used to give each sprinkling new as it touches gods hand before it touches the poor hands she explained.**

As she grow older and feel ill with Alzheimer there was no communication between us, I communicate

with her with love and compassion I had to groom her cut her nails be a mother and be at the hospital 6 am to start a case as she fall dying her room was full of 35 women reading Quran I was at the head of the body no tears were sheaf as the angles of mercy were present and would leave the place in the presence of tears. She was a lady of compassion, grace and kindness. Happy Mother's Day mom

About The Author

Dr. Alaa Zidan is an Orthopedic surgeon, a Professor in the Medical school, and a progressive thinker who is thriving to spread the message of saving human lives and unconditional love.

Into my Life is his second Book written in tribute to his late Sister, his First Book My own reflections was published on 2013 and it was well received internationally.

Authors Profile

Dr. Alaa Zidan is the Head of Training and creative Development NGN International (MENA Region) Kingdom of Bahrain from October 2015 till present Dr. Alaa Zidan was a consultant /Trainer in Health and Safety at the ALMashreq Training Centre, Bahrain from September 2011 till September 2o15 He was a Team leader in Sitra Health center, Ministry of Health Kingdom of Bahrain from March 2007 till June 2011, Alaa has 31 years of experience in emergency care, Trauma care and orthopedics and more than 10 years of teaching experience as a senior lecturer in the medical college, Arab gulf university Bahrain., he worked in different hospitals, university hospital in Alexandria Egypt, were he was graduated, Cairo university hospital where he had his master degree in orthopedics and trauma, he had his fellowship in trauma and fracture treatment from the Association of the study of internal fixation of fractures from the university hospital Freiburg, Germany and the university hospital of Bo chum Germany, Awarded SICOT scholarship in the Ricardo Galeazzi institute Milan, Italy.

Alaa has a wide experience in Emergency &Trauma care he worked as a deputy chief of emergency department in As Salam international hospital Cairo, Egypt, Senior Registrar orthopedics In Dr Fakhry hospital, Alkobar Saudi Arabia., senior registrar orthopedics in Salmanyia medical center, Bahrain, Chief Resident Emergency Salmanyia medical complex Bahrain. Alaa is an Advanced &Basic cardiac life support (ACLS) & (BLS) instructor for experienced health care providers Regional faculty of American heart association (AHA) Regional faculty and a professional premium member of the American Heart &Stroke Association; Member of the council of Basic cardiovascular sciences interdisciplinary working group on Quality of care &outcome Research, he taught plenty of ACLS and BLS courses with the American heart association as well as advanced first aid courses Alaa joined the National safety council in Chicago(NSC)since 2007, were he taught plenty of NSC standard first aid, CPR&AED courses in Bahrain, Saudi Arabia, Kuwait, and Russia where he was training the trainers for Emergency care on behalf of the NSC and he recently. become a certified Principles of occupational safety and health (POSH)&safety management techniques (SMT) instructor. Alaa moderated several important sessions during the international conference and Expo of the NSC, Orlando Florida, 2009

Session(s):

Elements of a Successful Office Ergonomics Program Environmental Regulations - An Overview for Beginners Communication Skills for a Crisis

In view of his vast experience and his passion and energy in teaching he became The NSC non exclusive representative in Emergency care in the Gulf cooperation council (GCC) and Middle East.

Alaa became a certified energy healer by earning his Diploma in Energy healing from the Institute of psychic energies Australia August 2009 in view of his extreme interest in the field of energy healing since 2006, and he master different techniques of energy healing such as Emotional freedom techniques(EFT), Quantum touch, healing touch, chakra activation ..etc.

Appointed as the course director of American heart association (AHA) Advanced cardiac life support (ACLS) course in Bahrain October 2010,

_____ _____

_____

Appointed By the NSC as A Defensive Driving Course 8/6 Instructor January 2011.

Alaa became a REIKI master, as he satisfactory completed the request course of study, demonstrated comprehension of REIKI principles and practices and being suitable character, has been empowered to and hereby conferred title of REIKI MASTER ON April 2011, Alaa Become a certified Master PR actioner in neurolinguistic programming (NLP) and certified Master life coach from the American university of NLP on 2011.

Awarded the Degree of Doctor of Philosophy in Occupational health and Safety from the OLford Walters University U.S.A May 2011, Awarded his second Ph.D. in Health education from CAMBELL University USA, January 2012 Awarded his third degree of Doctor of Philosophy Ph.D. in Behavioral Safety from McGraw University USA May 2012. Delivered a presentation about **Emotional**

intelligence and leadership skills in the National safety council Conference and Expo Orlando Florida 2012 which was well received and gained a lot of admiration. Alaa has been certified from the Energy medicine institute and Inner source in

distant learning course of Introduction to Energy medicine, overview, Energy Techniques and Energy Tracker on 2013.

Alaa Since 2011 is a Certified **NEBOSH** Instructor Delivering **NEBOSH Health and Safety Award Course (Level 2), NEBOSH IGC and NEBOSH Diploma Unit A and B** and also Alaa Is Certified **IOSH** Instructor delivering IOSH Working Safely and IOSH Managing Safely

Delivered another Presentation about Emotional Intelligence and Positive safety culture in the National safety council conference and Expo Chicago 2013 which was again well received and impressed the audience.

http://www.ishn.com/articles/print/96972-a-most-unusual-safety-session

Alaa Became a certified Engineering construction Industry training Board**(ECTIB)** Instructor for Basic, advanced &Supervisor **ECTIB** Courses on December 2013, His first contribution in 2014 was organizing and conducting a two days workshop on **Beyond Behavioral Based Safety** in ASSE Conference March 2014 in Bahrain and he Presented a stunning paper **about Connecting Emotional Intelligence to Success** this presentation was Extremely praised by the audience in view of its content and presenting style.

Recently, Alaa was Awarded with distinction a certificate in Inspiring Leadership through Emotional Intelligence from Case Western Reserve University, Cleveland, OHIO, USA.